THE KILLERS DAY & AGE

D1418961

WISE PUBLICATIONS
PART OF THE MUSIC SALES GROUP
LONDON/NEW YORK/PARIS/SYDNEY/COPENHAGEN/BERLIN/MADRID/TOKYO

PUBLISHED BY
WISE PUBLICATIONS,
14-15 BERNERS STREET, LONDON W1T 3LJ, UK.

EXCLUSIVE DISTRIBUTORS:
MUSIC SALES LIMITED, DISTRIBUTION CENTRE,
NEWMARKET ROAD, BURY ST EDMUNDS, SUFFOLK IP33 3YB, UK.

MUSIC SALES PTY LIMITED, 20 RESOLUTION DRIVE,
CARINGBAH, NSW 2229, AUSTRALIA.

ORDER NO. AM996798
ISBN 978-1-84772-992-7

THIS BOOK © COPYRIGHT 2009 WISE PUBLICATIONS,
A DIVISION OF MUSIC SALES LIMITED.

MUSIC ARRANGED BY DEREK JONES.
MUSIC PROCESSED BY PAUL EWERS MUSIC DESIGN.
EDITED BY FIONA BOLTON.

ARTWORK/PAINTINGS BY PAUL NORMANSELL.
ORIGINAL PACKAGE DESIGN: JULIAN PEPLOE STUDIO.

PRINTED IN THE EU.

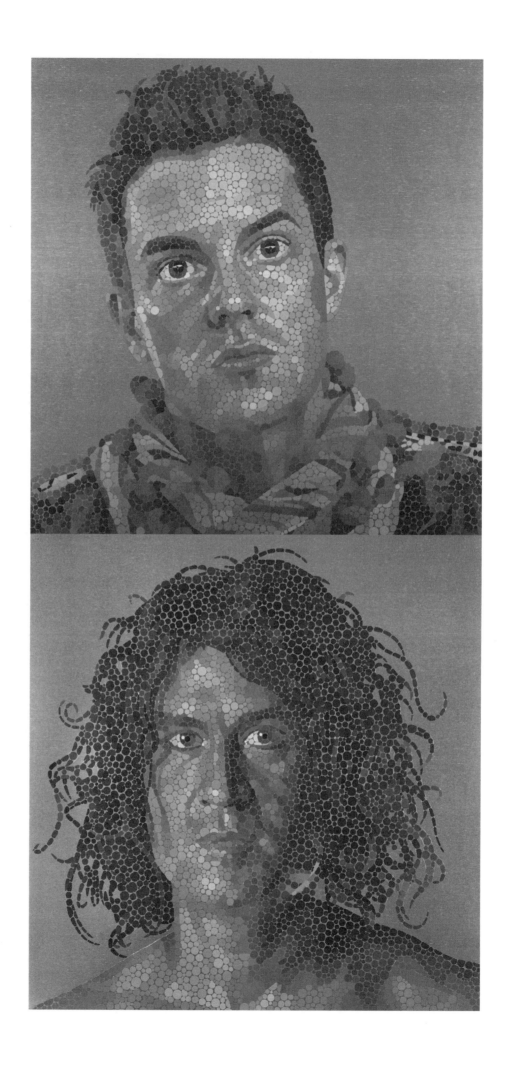

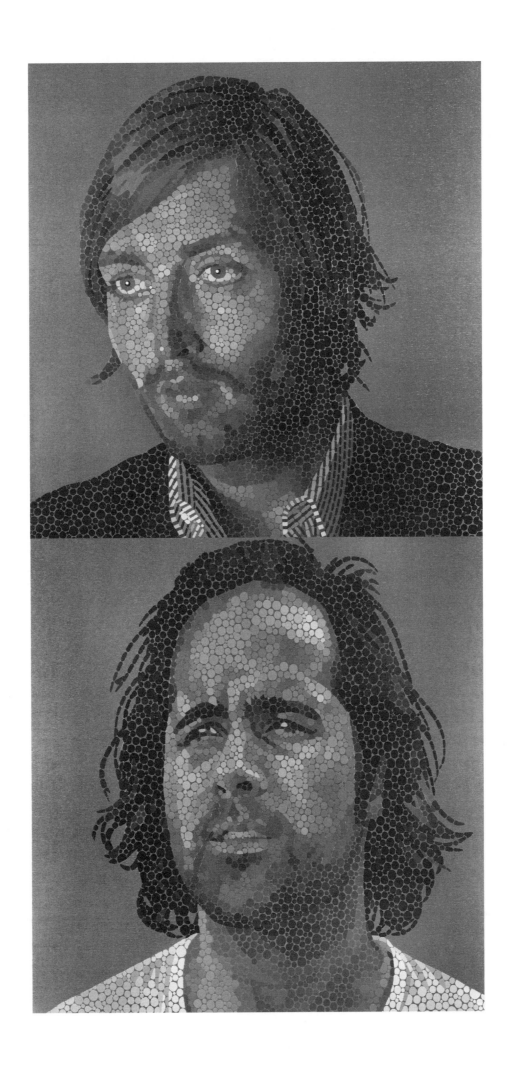

LOSING TOUCH

Lyrics by Brandon Flowers

Music by Brandon Flowers, Dave Keuning,

Mark Stoermer & Ronnie Vannucci

A⁵   D⁵

1. Con-sole me in my dark - est hour,   con-vince me that the
2. Con-sole me in my dark - est hour   then tell me that you

A⁵

truth is al - ways grey.   Ca - ress me in your vel - vet chair,
al - ways hear my cries.   I won-der what you've got con - spired,

D⁵   F

con-ceal me from the ghost you cast a - way.   }   I ain't in no hur-
I'm sure it dons a con - so - la - tion prize. }

C   G   Am

- ry, you go run and tell your friends I'm los - ing touch.

10

HUMAN

Lyrics by Brandon Flowers

Music by Brandon Flowers, Dave Keuning,
Mark Stoermer & Ronnie Vannucci

1. I did my best to no - tice when the call came down the line.___ Up to the plat - form of sur - ren-

(2.) -spects to grace and vir - tue, send my con- -do - len - ces to good.___ Give my re - gards to soul and ro-

still beat - ing? Are we hu - man or are we dan -

- cer? My sign is vi - tal, my hands are cold.

And I'm on my knees__ look - ing for the an - swer.__

You've got - ta let me know

SPACEMAN

Lyrics by Brandon Flowers

Music by Brandon Flowers, Dave Keuning,
Mark Stoermer & Ronnie Vannucci

23

The star-mak-er says it ain't so bad. The dream-mak-er's gon-na make you mad.

The space-man says ev-'ry-bod-y look down. It's all in your mind.

Effects

My glo-bal pos-i-tion sys-tems are vo-cal-ly ad-dressed.

They say the Nile_ used_ to run__ from east to west.__

They say the Nile_ used_ to run__ from east to west._

__ I'm__ fine, but I hear those___ voic - es at

night, some - time.

JOY RIDE

Lyrics by Brandon Flowers

**Music by Brandon Flowers, Dave Keuning,
Mark Stoermer & Ronnie Vannucci**

A DUSTLAND FAIRYTALE

Lyrics by Brandon Flowers
Music by Brandon Flowers, Dave Keuning,
Mark Stoermer & Ronnie Vannucci

40

THIS IS YOUR LIFE

Lyrics by Brandon Flowers

Music by Brandon Flowers, Dave Keuning,

Mark Stoermer & Ronnie Vannucci

Can - dy talks_ to stran - gers. Thinks her life's_ in dan - ger.

No - one gives a damn_ a - bout_ her hair. It's

I CAN'T STAY

Lyrics by Brandon Flowers
Music by Brandon Flowers, Dave Keuning,
Mark Stoermer & Ronnie Vannucci

53

NEON TIGER

Lyrics by Brandon Flowers

Music by Brandon Flowers, Dave Keuning,

Mark Stoermer & Ronnie Vannucci

Give me roll-ing hills_ and to-night could be the night that I stand a-mong the thou-sand thrills.

Mis-ter, cut me some slack_'cause I don't wan-na go back. I want a new day and age._

Come on girls_ and boys,_ ev-'ry-one make some noise._

D.S. al Coda

57

THE WORLD WE LIVE IN

Lyrics by Brandon Flowers

Music by Brandon Flowers, Dave Keuning,
Mark Stoermer & Ronnie Vannucci

that we live in.   I had a dream and   I was fall-

-ing   down.

There's no   next time a-lone.____   A storm wastes_ it's wa-ter on me.__

____   But my   life   was

GOODNIGHT, TRAVEL WELL

Lyrics by Brandon Flowers
Music by Brandon Flowers, Dave Keuning,
Mark Stoermer & Ronnie Vannucci

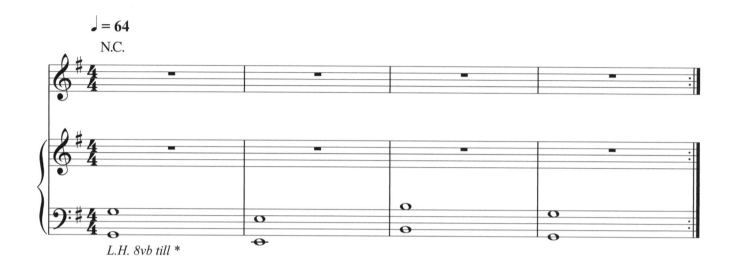

The un-known dis-tance to the great beyond stares back at my griev-ing frame.

To cast my shad-ow by the ho - ly sun, my spi-rit moans

123456789